GREGORY L. VOGT

# NEPTUNE

The Millbrook Press
Brookfield, Connecticut

ɣ wM

Published by The Millbrook Press
2 Old New Milford Road
Brookfield, Connecticut 06804

Library of Congress Cataloging-in-Publication Data

Vogt, Gregory.
Neptune / Gregory L. Vogt.
p.   cm.—(Gateway solar system)
Includes bibliographical references and index.
Summary: An introduction to Neptune, eighth planet from the sun.
ISBN 1-56294-331-6 (lib. bdg.)
1. Neptune (Planet)—Juvenile literature.   [1. Neptune (Planet)]
I. Title.   II. Series: Vogt, Gregory. Gateway solar system.
QB691.V64   1993
523.4′81—dc20        92-30183   CIP   AC

Photographs and illustrations courtesy National Aeronautics
and Space Administration

Solar system diagram by Anne Canevari Green

# NEPTUNE

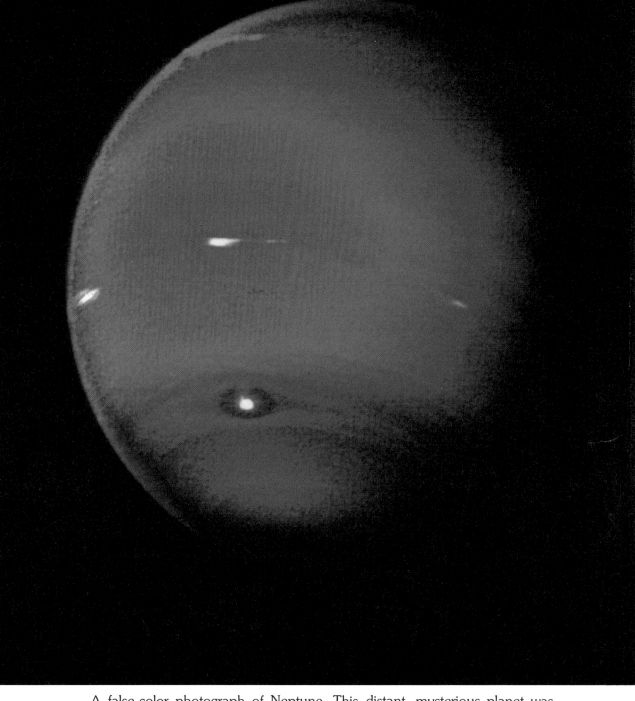

A false-color photograph of Neptune. This distant, mysterious planet was unknown in ancient times.

In the early 1800s, no one knew that the planet Neptune existed. Most people believed that our solar system was made up of the sun, seven planets, and several moons. But *astronomers*—scientists who study objects in outer space—were not so sure.

The astronomers thought that at least one other planet might be *orbiting* (traveling around) the sun. They had been studying the distant planet Uranus. And what they saw was very odd.

They knew how far Uranus was from the sun. And they had figured out how fast the planet *should* travel on its orbit around the sun. But Uranus didn't act as they predicted. For years, the planet moved slightly faster than expected. Then it slowed down. Uranus never moved exactly as the astronomers thought it would.

What could make Uranus speed up and slow down in this way? Maybe a powerful force was pulling on Uranus, causing its speed to change. That force might be *gravity*—the force that causes objects to attract each other.

Gravity is a very powerful force. It is gravity that keeps you and all the other objects on Earth from flying off into space. The gravitational pull of an unknown planet could be strong enough to make Uranus speed up and slow down.

## The Search for Neptune

In the 1840s a young English scientist named John Couch Adams decided to find this mysterious unknown planet. But he didn't use a telescope. Instead, he began his search with mathematics. Adams used measurements of Uranus's movements to figure out where the unknown planet might be.

After four years, Adams had completed his work. He showed his calculations to the astronomer royal at the Greenwich Observatory, outside London. But Adams was young and inexperienced. Other scientists did not take his work seriously.

Meanwhile, a French scientist was also trying to figure out where the mystery planet might be. Urbain Jean Joseph Le Verrier published his own calculations. He and Adams did not know of each other's work. But their conclusions were very much alike.

Both scientists thought the mystery planet would be found in the same general area. Because of this, scientists looked more closely at Adams's work. Astronomers

Pluto ————————————————————————————

Neptune ————————————————————

Uranus ——————————————

Saturn ——————————————

Jupiter ——————

Mars ——

Earth ——

Venus ——

Mercury ——

SUN

combed the night sky with their telescopes. The search for the mystery planet was on.

Finally, on September 23, 1846, the planet was spotted. Johann Gottfried Galle of the Berlin Observatory in Germany found it very near the place Adams and Le Verrier had thought it would be. The newfound planet was named Neptune.

## The Eighth Planet

Neptune is a cold, dark world. It is cold and dark because it is very far from the sun—nearly 2 billion 800 million miles (4.5 billion kilometers). This is 30 times the distance between Earth and the sun. At this distance, the sun appears as just a bright star. The sun is 900 times brighter in Earth's sky than it is in Neptune's sky.

Being so far out in space, Neptune must travel a very large orbit. Thus a Neptune year—the amount of time it takes the planet to travel once around the sun—is very long. The planet takes almost 165 Earth years to complete its orbit. If you were born on Neptune and

◀ The *Voyager 2* spacecraft took this picture of Neptune from 9.2 million miles (14.8 million km) away.

lived to be 100 Earth years old, you would still be 65 Earth years away from your first Neptune birthday!

A Neptune year may be very long, but a Neptune day is short. This distant planet takes just a bit more than 16 hours to spin once on its *axis* (an imaginary line running through the planet from its north pole to its south pole).

Neptune is the fourth and smallest of the four giant gas planets in our solar system. (The others are Jupiter, Saturn, and Uranus.) It is 30,776 miles (49,528 kilometers) in diameter. That makes the planet four times larger in diameter than Earth is. If Neptune were a hollow ball, 60 Earths could fit inside it.

Neptune can be thought of as the twin planet of Uranus. Uranus is only about 1,000 miles (1,600 kilometers) larger in diameter. And both planets are nearly the same color—blue.

Like Uranus, Neptune is made up mainly of gas. And like all the giant gas planets, Neptune has an atmosphere with a thick layer of hydrogen and helium gas.

Bright clouds are seen in the northern sky of Neptune. High-speed winds, ▶ moving as fast as 1,500 miles (2,400 km) per hour, stretch the clouds out in long streaks.

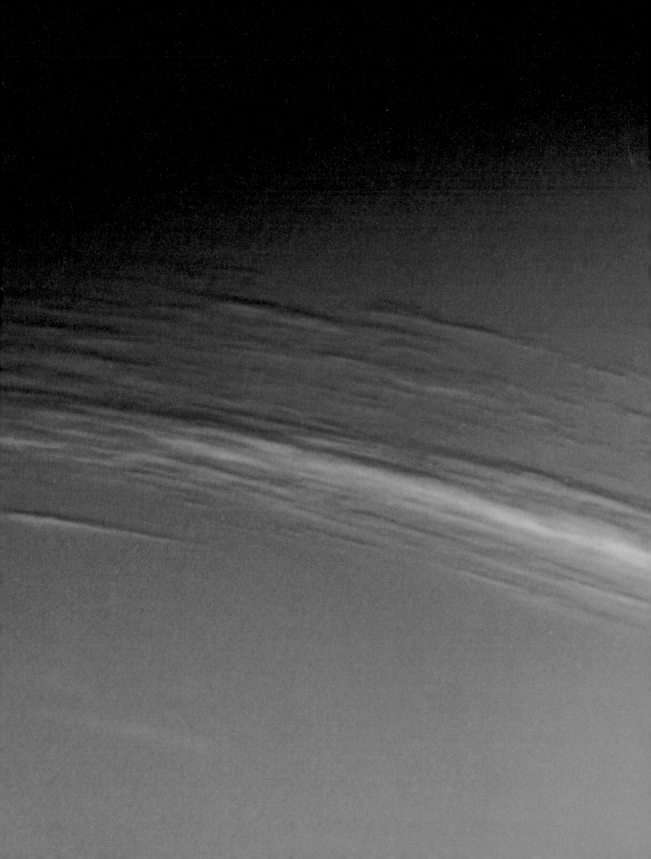

Beneath these gases is a liquid interior, with a core of rock and metal.

Also like Uranus, Neptune has large amounts of methane gas in its atmosphere. The methane gives Neptune its blue color. Methane gas absorbs the reds, oranges, and yellows of the rainbow colors in sunlight. Only the blues are left to reflect back into space.

## Many Surprises

Until 1989, scientists thought that Neptune was a rather dull planet. But in that year, they received surprising information about Neptune.

The information came from a very special spacecraft, *Voyager 2*. *Voyager 2* had been launched from Earth in 1977 by the National Aeronautics and Space Administration (NASA). It had flown past Jupiter, Saturn, and Uranus, and in 1989 it reached Neptune. *Voyager 2* thus became the first spacecraft to visit all four of the giant gas planets. It is still the only spacecraft to have done so.

When *Voyager 2* passed by Jupiter, it recorded much turbulence—storms, winds, and other activity—in the planet's atmosphere. Bands of colored gases were sweeping around the planet at high speed. Jupiter's *Great*

An artist's view of *Voyager 2* as it headed toward Neptune. The spacecraft had already visited Saturn and Jupiter, seen in the background.

*Red Spot* was shown to be a storm three times larger than the planet Earth itself.

The view of Saturn's atmosphere was less exciting. Its bands were fainter, and its spots were smaller. Ura-

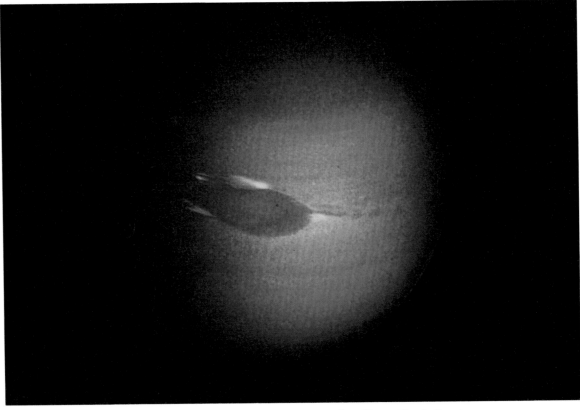

Clouds in Neptune's atmosphere swirl about to create the Great Dark Spot.

nus was duller still. So as *Voyager 2* approached Neptune, scientists were not expecting much. They thought that the farther a planet was from the sun, the colder and more sluggish its atmosphere would be.

Neptune surprised them all. The cameras and scientific instruments aboard *Voyager 2* made many important discoveries.

Neptune has its own great spot. The spot is very dark, instead of bright red like Jupiter's spot. *Voyager 2* scientists called Neptune's spot the *Great Dark Spot.* Like Jupiter's spot, it is a huge hurricane-like storm that spins counterclockwise. As it spins, the storm moves westward across the planet at a speed of almost 745 miles (1,200 kilometers) an hour.

*Voyager 2* also discovered a second, smaller spot. And the spacecraft found a small, fast-moving white cloud that scientists nicknamed "scooter." Wind speeds on Neptune were clocked at as high as 1,500 miles (2,400 kilometers) an hour. These were the fastest winds of any planet in the solar system.

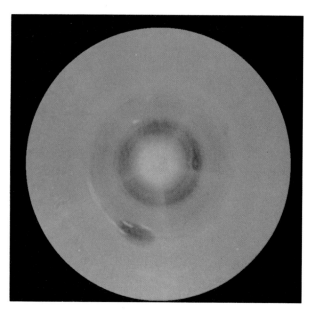

*Voyager 2*'s path led the spacecraft under the south pole of Neptune. The ring around the pole is a band of dark clouds that stretch completely around the planet. An oval-shaped storm can also be seen.

Scientists also learned that the methane gas in Neptune's atmosphere is constantly being recycled. High in the atmosphere, sunlight causes the methane to break down, forming other gases and tiny specks called haze particles. The haze particles sink into the lower atmosphere, where they meet up with hydrogen. The result is a chemical reaction that creates more methane. And the methane is carried back to the upper atmosphere by Neptune's violent winds.

## Ring Arcs

*Voyager 2* also helped clear up a mystery about Neptune. The mystery had begun back in 1981, when astronomers had known that Neptune was going to pass in front of a distant star. They had hoped this event would help them make a discovery about Neptune.

Four years earlier, Uranus had also passed in front of a star. That star's light had blinked off and on five times before Uranus blocked it. It blinked five more times as Uranus moved to the other side of the star. The blinking meant that something had gotten in the way of the star's light. The astronomers had discovered rings encircling Uranus.

Would the star Neptune was going to pass in front

"Ring arcs" around Neptune are really continuous rings. Some areas of the rings are too faint to be easily seen.

of also blink? To the delight of the astronomers, the star did blink. Astronomers knew then that Neptune also has rings. That meant that all four of the giant gas planets have rings.

But there was something different about Neptune's

rings. The rings did not appear to be complete circles, so astronomers called them *ring arcs.* The ring arcs mystified the astronomers, because planetary rings should be evenly spread out around a planet. What would cause these rings to exist in pieces?

A partial answer came with *Voyager 2's* visit. It sent back pictures that showed the rings were complete circles after all. Like other planetary rings, they were made up of billions of tiny particles, all circling the planet. But some segments of the rings were so thin and made up of such fine particles that they were hard to see from Earth.

## Neptune's Moons

Within one month of the discovery of Neptune, a British astronomer spotted the largest of Neptune's moons, or *satellites,* and named it Triton. (A satellite is a small body that orbits a larger body in space. Moons are "natural satellites" that orbit planets. Orbiting spacecraft are sometimes called "artificial satellites" because they are made by people.) Triton, 1,678 miles (2,700 kilometers) in diameter, is about three quarters of the size of Earth's moon.

After careful study, astronomers made an interest-

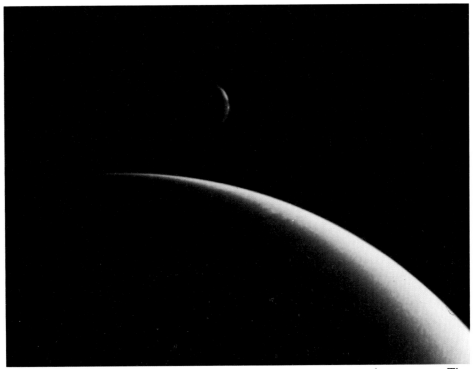

Triton, Neptune's largest moon, is the smaller crescent in this picture. The moon is in front of and above Neptune.

ing discovery. Triton is a "backward" moon. Unlike nearly every other moon in the solar system, Triton orbits its planet in a direction opposite from the planet's direction of *rotation*. (Rotation is the spinning of a planet around its axis.)

This led astronomers to suppose that Triton is not a natural moon of Neptune. Instead, Triton was probably a stray body in our solar system that passed near

Neptune several billion years ago. If conditions were right, the gravitation between these two bodies could have captured Triton, causing it to orbit Neptune.

Unfortunately for Triton, its orbit around Neptune is decaying. In other words, Triton is getting closer to Neptune. At present, Triton orbits Neptune at a distance of 220,469 miles (354,800 kilometers). But, in a few billion years, Triton will get so close to Neptune that the

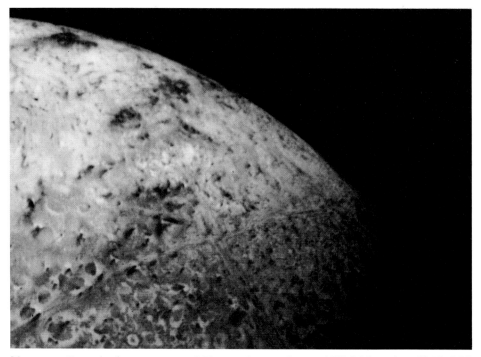

*Voyager 2* took this picture of Triton from about 130,000 miles (210,000 km) away. The moon is shown in its natural color. Many craters can be seen, and two cracks cross in the middle of the picture.

force of gravitation will tear Triton apart. The fragments of Triton will then form a huge ring encircling Neptune.

Triton has its own atmosphere. For this to happen, a moon or planet must have a strong gravitational pull— to keep the gas from escaping into space. Triton's atmosphere is very thin. At least part of the atmosphere comes from geyser eruptions that spew out invisible nitrogen gas and dusty particles. The nitrogen may form thin clouds a few miles above the surface.

At Triton's surface the temperature is about 391 degrees below zero Fahrenheit ($-235$ degrees Celsius). This probably makes Triton the coldest place in the solar system.

Triton's surface shows two different types of land. Part of it is an icecap, and part looks like the skin of a cantaloupe. The icecap surface is probably made of frozen nitrogen and methane gases. In places, dark streaks cross the icecap. The streaks are the fallout of dusty particles from the geysers.

Triton seems to have the same general size and chemical makeup as the planet Pluto. No spacecraft has ever been sent to Pluto, and none is even in the planning stages. So Triton is being used by astronomers as a model of what Pluto may be like.

Before the arrival of *Voyager 2*, astronomers knew

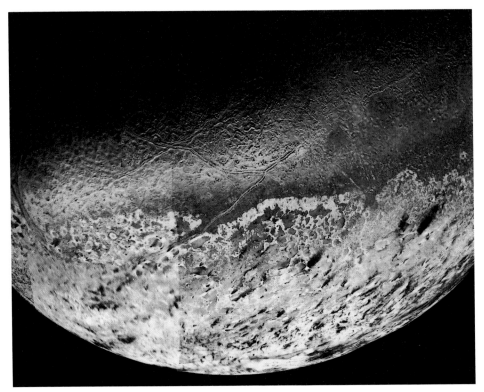

About 12 *Voyager* photos of Triton were combined to make this picture of Neptune's largest moon. The south polar region appears to be covered with nitrogen ice. An area of light, almost bluish material runs across the middle of the picture, and cracks and craters can be seen clearly.

of only one more moon circling Neptune. This was Nereid, which is 211 miles (340 kilometers) in diameter. It was discovered by astronomers in 1949. Nereid is the third largest of Neptune's moons.

Not much is known about Nereid because *Voyager 2* never came very close to this moon. The spacecraft did discover that Nereid reflects sunlight about as much as Earth's own moon does. Nereid has an orbit that is much more egg-shaped than any other moon in the solar system. When Nereid is at its farthest point from Neptune, it is 13 times farther than our moon is from Earth.

Little is known about Neptune's other moons. Six new moons were discovered by *Voyager 2*. None of these moons is round. The largest is Proteus, and the smallest is Naiad. Naiad is only 36 miles (58 kilometers) in diameter.

Proteus is larger than Nereid by about 47 miles (76

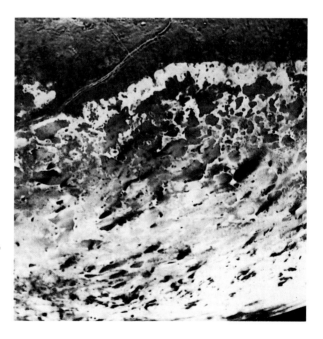

A close view of Triton's south polar region. The dark plumes may be ice volcanoes.

As *Voyager 2* headed past Neptune toward interstellar space, it took this picture of the planet's south polar region.

kilometers). You might expect that it would have been discovered before Nereid. But Proteus is much closer to Neptune than is Nereid. Because of that, Proteus was lost in the glare of the planet. Proteus is one of the darkest objects in the solar system. It is about as dark as the soot that comes from a candle flame.

## The Most Distant Planet

When *Voyager 2* passed Neptune in 1989, it sped out into deep space. There were no more planets left to visit on its outward voyage. This might seem odd because every astronomy book lists Pluto as the most distant planet.

For most of the Pluto year (248 Earth years) this is true. But Pluto's orbit is not circular. Once every Pluto year, the farthest planet dips inside Neptune's orbit. For about 20 Earth years, the eighth and ninth planets trade places. Then Pluto, now on its outward journey, passes outside Neptune's orbit and becomes the farthest planet again.

For the time being, Neptune is still the farthest planet from the Sun. It will be the farthest until 1999.

# NEPTUNE QUICK FACTS

Neptune: Named after the ancient Roman god of the sea.

|  | Neptune | Earth |
|---|---|---|
| *Average Distance From the Sun* | | |
| Millions of miles | 2,797 | 93 |
| Millions of kilometers | 4,501 | 150 |
| *Revolution (one orbit around the sun)* | *164.79 years* | *1 year* |
| *Average Orbital Speed* | | |
| Miles per second | 3.37 | 18.6 |
| Kilometers per second | 5.43 | 30 |
| *Rotation (spinning once)* | 16 hours, 7 minutes | 24 hours |
| *Diameter at Equator* | | |
| Miles | 30,776 | 7,926 |
| Kilometers | 49,528 | 12,756 |
| *Surface Gravity (compared to Earth's)* | 1.15 | 1 |
| *Mass (the amount of matter contained in Neptune, compared to Earth)* | 17.15 | 1 |
| *Atmosphere* | hydrogen, helium, methane | nitrogen, oxygen |
| *Satellites (moons)* | 8 | 1 |
| *Rings* | 5 | 0 |

| Neptune's Moons | Diameter* | Distance From Planet |
|---|---|---|
| Naiad | 36 mi | 29,970 mi |
| | 58 km | 48,230 km |
| Thalassa | 50 mi | 31,113 mi |
| | 80 km | 50,070 km |
| Despoina | 98 mi | 32,641 mi |
| | 158 km | 52,530 km |
| Galatea | 92 mi | 38,495 mi |
| | 148 km | 61,950 km |
| Larissa | 119 mi | 45,703 mi |
| | 192 km | 73,550 km |
| Proteus | 258 mi | 73,100 mi |
| | 416 km | 117,640 km |
| Triton | 1,678 mi | 220,469 mi |
| | 2,700 km | 354,800 km |
| Nereid | 211 mi | 3,423,896 mi |
| | 340 km | 5,509,100 km |

*Most of Neptune's moons aren't round. The largest dimension is given.

# GLOSSARY

| | |
|---|---|
| Astronomer | A scientist who studies planets, moons, stars, and other objects in outer space. |
| Axis | An imaginary line running through the planet from its north to its south pole. |
| Equator | An imaginary line running around the middle of a planet and halfway between the planet's north and south poles. |
| Gravity | A force that causes all objects to attract each other. |
| Great Dark Spot | A huge, dark oval-shaped storm in Neptune's atmosphere. |
| Great Red Spot | A reddish oval-shaped storm in Jupiter's atmosphere. |
| Mass | The amount of matter contained in an object. |
| Orbit | The path a planet takes to travel around the sun, or a moon to travel around a planet. |
| Revolution | One complete orbit of a planet around the sun, or a moon around a planet. |
| Ring arcs | The name given to Neptune's rings when astronomers thought the rings were incomplete. |
| Rotation | The spinning of a planet or moon around its axis. |
| Satellite | A small body in space that orbits around a larger body. A satellite may be "natural," as a moon, or "artificial," as a spacecraft. |
| Scooter | A fast-moving white cloud in Neptune's atmosphere. |
| *Voyager 2* | Spacecraft that visited Jupiter in 1979, flew by Saturn in 1981, Uranus in 1986, and Neptune in 1989. |

# FOR FURTHER READING

Asimov, I. *Neptune: The Farthest Giant.* Milwaukee: Gareth Stevens, 1990.

Gallant, R. *The Planets, Exploring the Solar System.* New York: Four Winds Press, 1982.

Landau, E. *Neptune.* New York: Franklin Watts, 1991.

Simon, S. *Neptune.* New York: William Morrow, 1991.

Vogt, G. *Voyager.* Brookfield, Conn.: The Millbrook Press, 1991.

# INDEX

# ABOUT THE AUTHOR

Gregory L. Vogt works for NASA's Education Division
at the Johnson Space Center in Houston, Texas.
He works with astronauts in developing educational
videos for schools.

Mr. Vogt previously served as executive director of the
Discovery World Museum of Science, Economics and
Technology in Milwaukee, Wisconsin, and as an eighth-
grade science teacher. He holds bachelor's and master's
degrees in science from the University of Wisconsin at
Milwaukee, as well as a doctorate in curriculum and
instruction from Oklahoma State University.